# EASTERN NAGALAND (FRONTIER NAGALAND) MOVEMENT

RITURAJ BASUMATARY

Made with ♥ on the Notion Press Platform
www.notionpress.com

# Contents

# PREFACE

This book deals with the movement for a separate state called Eastern Nagaland. Hope that the publication of this book will be useful for the readers. Enjoy reading.

# I
# Introduction

Tuensang is a town located in the north-eastern part of the Indian state of Nagaland. It is the headquarters of the Tuensang District and has a population of 36,774. The town was founded in 1947 for the purpose of administrating the erstwhile North Eastern Frontier Agency (NEFA) that comprised the present day Districts of Tuensang, Mon, Longleng, Kiphire, Noklak and Shamator. Today, these six districts combined are also known as 'Eastern Nagaland'.

# II
# History

The Tuensang area was originally made up of all the present six districts of Eastern Nagaland. Even after the British conquest of India, the Tuensang tribal region remained unadministered due to lack of sufficient men and money. However, in 1902, the area was brought under the nominal control of the British. It was called Tribal Area and was administered by the Governor General of India. In 1948, a separate division called Tuensang Administrative Circle was created.

When the Constitution of India was first released in 1950, Tuensang Division was placed in "Part B" category of tribal districts as per the Sixth Schedule. It became part of the North-East Frontier Agency (NEFA). Subsequently, in 1957, it was merged with the Naga Hills District to form a new administrative unit under the Ministry of External Affairs. After negotiation with the secessionists, this administrative unit was later made a full-fledged state called Nagaland.

# III

# Eastern Naga People's Organization

As the demand for "Frontier Nagaland" by the Eastern Naga People's Organization (ENPO) echoes, the apex body of the region is set to hold a crucial meeting with its elected representatives, tribal bodies, and federating units at the Konyak Union office in Mon on 16 November 2022.

ENPO President Tsapikiu Sangtam informed EastMojo that the main agenda of the meeting is with regard to their demand for a separate state.

Last month, i.e. on October 2022, the apex body of the Eastern Nagas had decided to demand the resignation of its 20 MLAs if the Government of India did not pay heed to its demand.

It had also reaffirmed its August 26, 2022, resolution where it adopted a resolution of 'not taking part in any election process of the central and state goernment until and unless a separate statehood is granted by the Government of India, as demanded by the people of Eastern Nagaland under the aegis of ENPO'.

It said that with no early response from the Central government towards its demand for separate statehood, the demand for the resignation of 20 legislators representing Eastern Nagas at the Nagaland Legislative Assembly (NLA) will be made along with the resignation of all political party workers, both at the central and regional level.

Seven tribal bodies, including the Chang Khulei Setshang (CKS), Khiamniungan Tribal Council (KTC), Konyak Union (KU), Phom People's Council (PPC), United Sangtam Likhum Pumji (USLP), Tikhir Tribal Council (TTC) and Yimkhiung Tribal Council (YTC) had endorsed the resolution.

It had also adopted a resolution to abstain from participating in the annual Hornbill Festival at Kisama, Kohima, from this year i.e. 2022 onwards due to the hardships faced by the participants.

The Central Executive Council (CEC) meeting is scheduled to take the Statehood Demand movement way forward.

The ENPO has also invited any like-minded ENPO members to attend the CEC meeting with proper consultation with their respective Tribal Bodies.

An official of the Konyak Union (KU) informed that around 300 people will be attending the meeting.

# IV

# Eastern Nagaland (Frontier Nagaland) Movement

The Eastern Nagaland area presently comprises of six districts namely; Tuensang, Mon, Kiphire, Longleng, Noklak and Shamator. The whole area is inhabited by seven major tribes such as Sangtam, Chang, Konyak, Yimkhiung, Khiamniungan, Phom and Tikhirs and very little population of Sumis. The Tuensang town serves as a nerve center of the eastern part of Nagaland. All this area remained totally unadministered in the pre-independence days and so the British had declared it as excluded area. The region was left outside the 'innerline', a bureaucratic division separating tea gardens and other areas of commercial interest for the colonial government in the Northeast from areas that were unadministered or partially administered. In 1948, for the first time, an administrative centre was established at Tuensang . In 1945 the entire Naga

Hill areas including eastern Nagaland was brought under the Northeast Frontier Agency (NEFA). In 1957, the Tuensang Frontier Division (Eastern Region) was separated from the NEFA and merged with the Naga Hills District of Assam to form a new administrative unit called the Naga Hills Tuensang Area. The administration of NHTA was the responsibility of the Governor of Assam under the control of the Ministry of External Affairs, Government of India. There were only three districts at that time in Nagaland ie, Kohima, Mokokchung and Tuensang. It was under the banner of Naga Hills Tuensang Area, on 1st December 1963 a full-fledged state of 'Nagaland 'was created as the 16th state of the Indian Union.

Special provisions were made for the then Tuensang District in view of its relative backwardness, under which the district would have a Regional Council of its own for a period of Ten years with the Deputy Commissioner as chairman. The Regional Council also nominated tribal representatives to be the member of the Nagaland Legislative Assembly. There was a separate Ministry for Tuensang affairs from amongst the nominated members of the area. However in 1973, at the end of the ten year period the Regional Council was abolished and the people of Tuensang District began to participate in the elections to the Nagaland Legislative Assembly along with the rest of the state. The Region became just another part of state without any special provision and was subsequently divided into Districts like Tuensang, Mon, Kiphire, Longleng, Noklak and Shamator.

Even in the legal point of view, the constitution of India 1949 under article 371 A speaks about special provision with respect to state of Nagaland. Article 371 clause 2(b), has a special mention that where any money is provided by the

Government of India to the Government of Nagaland to meet the requirements of the state of Nagaland as a whole, the Governor shall in his discretion arrange for an equitable allocation of that money between the Tuensang district and the rest of the state. Has this provision really got implemented?

It is generally aware of the fact that the fruits of development have not reached the common men and women. This is true, in the areas under eastern Nagaland where the region is yet to see the light of the day. There is a big development gap and this is the core of the issue. While policies and programmes do exist, it is the 'governance deficit' which has contributed to the present day problem. It is not just that development programmes or government funds are lacking but simply the fact that these have not been implemented properly. Clearly, the present State (Nagaland) has failed to deliver the goods to the people. This is the verdict coming out of the Eastern Nagaland Peoples Organisation grievances. There is a growing demand for. It is something for the State government to gloss over and try and find some answers quickly.

# V
# Tuensang

Tuensang is one of the larger towns in Nagaland along with Chümoukedima, Dimapur, Kohima and Mokokchung. The landowners/permanent tribes of the town are mainly the Changs, Sangtams, Yimkhiungs and Khiamniungans. The town serves as a nerve center for the eastern part of Nagaland.

Tuensang is the headquarters to apex organisations such as Eastern Nagaland Peoples' Organisation (ENPO), Eastern Naga Students' Federation (ENSF), Khiamniungan Tribal Council (KTC), Chang Khulei Setshang (CKS), Confederation of Chang Students' Union (CCSU), Chang Baptist Lashong Thangyen (CBLT), Eleutheros Christian Society (ECS), Eastern Farming Association, etc.

# VI
## Conclusion

The Eastern Nagas were almost half a century behind the other Naga brothers. The reason why the whole Eastern Nagas accepted the Christian Missionaries and embraced the Christian faith was solely out of hope and trust that Nagas as one Christian family will be able to work together and progress together in life. However in the process, the Eastern Naga tribes had to suffer a lot and is still suffering from that association. Eastern people have not received much benefits from that friendship with the advanced Naga tribes. Since the Nagas of Naga Hills were advanced in the field of Education, even grade IV jobs in the Eastern Naga areas were being filled up by the educated ones. The job that was created were all taken away by the advanced brothers. The educated leaders and government bureaucrats took advantage of the eastern areas, which led to the wide disparity among the family. After the statehood, Tuensang was not under Nagaland State Assembly but had a Regional Council of its own which was kept under External Affairs. The huge amounts meant for the development of Eastern Areas are siphoned off by people in power. People who get posted in eastern areas takes it as an opportunity to give backward excuses, relax and then take away anything that is meant for the development of the villages. Even after sixty years of statehood there are many villages untouched by modernity. There are many who are yet to see the fruits of development of the present statehood. The employment in the state has grossed more than one lakh and the percentage of Eastern Nagas employed in the government sector is too less. The successive government keeps on creating vacant posts in the backward areas by allowing the government employees posted in the eastern villages to be transferred along with the posts to other towns. This is the major reason why the government schools in the villages are existing and running without sufficient teachers.

Those that have not ventured out of their hearth may say that all are being treated equally but those who visited the Eastern Areas get to see the reality being so appalled by the living conditions of the villagers. One can't even imagine that the eastern villagers are economically so poor even to feed their children forget about educating them. It is not surprising thing to see so many children from eastern areas working in others house to work as maids and servants.

The data published by DUDA-department of state government under the title "Eastern Nagaland at a glance" shows that there is a vast gap that exists between the eastern districts with the rest of the state on all the development metrics. The literacy rate are much lower and the unemployment rate is significantly high and the health infrastructure is in a very bad shape. It is a known fact that the funds meant for the development of the state is siphoned off by people in power of both the backward and advanced tribes for their own benefit. Despite all the circumstances stated above, there is still a ray of hope for the people of the region to govern themselves once a popular demand for creation of 'Frontier Nagaland' state is achieved.

www.ingramcontent.com/pod-product-compliance
Lightning Source LLC
Chambersburg PA
CBHW071259140726
47996CB00007B/2916